MW00416092

SHOES

SHOES

By Raissa Bretaña

A TINY FOLIO™
Abbeville Press Publishers
New York London

Front cover: *Evening pumps*, Spring 2016. Roger Vivier, French, founded 1937. Silk satin with rhinestone buckle.

Back cover: *Latchet shoe*, 1760–80. British. Patterned silk upper and covered Louis heel trimmed with metallic braid; leather sole. See page 55.

Spine: *Evening slipper*, 1860–70. British. Silk satin upper with ribbon stripes and rosettes. See page 108.

Endpapers (front): *Sandals*, c. 1949. Delman, American, founded 1919. Multicolored suede. See page 190.

Endpapers (back): *Sandals*, c. 1950. Seymour Troy Originals, American. Leather. See page 188.

Page 2: *Evening pumps*, 1908–14. Charles Lee, British. Gold patent leather with Louis heel.

Page 6: John Ferrell. *Washington, DC. Shoe store window on F Street,* 1942 (detail). Library of Congress, Washington, DC.

Page 10: *Chopines*, 1550–1650. Italian. Silk velvet trimmed with gold lace, hobnails, metallic braid, shirred ribbon, and tassels.

Page 30: *Latchet shoes with jeweled buckle*, 1740–50. English. Silk damask upper; latchets fastened with metal buckle featuring cut-paste stones; leather sole.

Page 64: *Evening slippers*, 1845–65. Hobbs, British. Silk satin upper with fringed trim and ribbon laces.

Page 96: *High-button boots*, c. 1895. American. Leather upper with cutout vamp design and button closure.

Page 130: *Evening shoes*, c. 1927. A la Gavotte, French. Patterned metallic-silk upper with covered heel and embellished rhinestone straps.

Page 168: *Platform peep-toe sandals*, 1940s. Revelers, American. Silk satin and gilt-leather upper; wood heel and leather sole.

Page 206: *Slingback shoes*, 1965. Designed for the House of Charles Jourdan, French, founded 1919. Patent leather and heel.

Page 244: *Peep-toe stiletto bootie*, 2004. Yves Saint Laurent, French, founded 1961. Leather upper covered with feathers.

CONTENTS

INTRODUCTION

For the past four hundred years, women's footwear has evolved in tandem with fashionable dress—reflecting both the aesthetic principles and social conventions of each era. At various points throughout modern history, shoes have become the focal point of style, power, status, and sexuality. From the luxuriously embellished heels of the Rococo, to the demure slippers of the early nineteenth century, to the towering platform pumps of the new millennium—cultural affiliations with each style have emerged to effectively chronicle women's social history through fashionable footwear. Though comfort and practicality will always have a place in design and commerce, the shoe's narrative ultimately culminates in the triumph of style over mere function.

Shoes have long been considered an essential component of a fashionable ensemble—acting as the definitive punctuation on a complete look, whether or not immediately visible. Footwear design has historically corresponded to the rise and fall of hemlines across the centuries. In earlier instances (throughout the seventeenth to the nineteenth centuries), highly decorative shoes were concealed beneath long skirts and treasured as more intimate objects of luxury. By the twentieth century, shortened skirts meant feet were on full display, and eye-catching shoes figured prominently in dress practices. Just as the aesthetics of fashionable dress were influenced by prevailing tastes in art and architecture, shoes often bore visual characteristics seen in the decorative arts. Hallmarks of Baroque, Neoclassical, and Art Deco design were reflected in the design of footwear of each corresponding era. Postmodernism promoted the revival of historical styles in the late twentieth century, while some silhouettes—like the classic pump—have become mainstays.

The production and consumption of shoes have evolved in response to a footwear industry that has become increasingly mechanized. Where shoes had been individually handmade by a skilled cobbler for the better part of the seventeenth and eighteenth centuries, they were produced on a more prolific scale due to the arrival of industrialization in the nineteenth. Such developments made fashionable footwear more widely accessible, which led retail markets to flourish as they grew to accommodate changing consumer behaviors. The height of shoe manufacturing in America lasted from about 1870 to 1930—coinciding with the rise of the American department store and the mail-order catalog. The steady trend toward mass production in the twentieth century has led to a gradual increase in the number of shoes necessary to complete a standard wardrobe. Several studies in recent years have shown that women own around twenty pairs on average—while some proudly boast much more vast collections.

Indeed, shoes have become the frequent object of obsession for fashion enthusiasts of the twenty-first century. Historically, footwear had been relegated to the role of accessory—a supplemental item intended to support a fashionable garment—however, shoes have since become significant objects of desire in their own right. Despite the undeniable increase of mass-manufacturing, an appetite for craftsmanship has continued to support a robust luxury footwear industry. Designers have never ceased to experiment with form and concept—continuously pushing the boundary of what a shoe can be. With technological developments in materials and fabrication, some have even turned shoes into stand-alone art objects that are more akin to sculpture than wearable footwear.

This volume illustrates the evolution of women's fashionable footwear over the course of four centuries using 250 of the finest examples selected from museum collections, including the Metropolitan Museum of Art, the Victoria and Albert Museum, the Museum at FIT, and the Museum of Fine Arts, Boston. Whether practical, fantastical, comfortable, or collectible, these shoes recount the history of footwear design and the fashionable female experience.

CHAPTER ONE
17th Century

Fashionable dress during the seventeenth century was influenced by the ornate grandeur of Baroque-era aesthetics in art, architecture, and design. Throughout this period, women's fashion consisted of gowns and mantuas with long, trailing skirts that concealed the feet. In the canal city of Venice—a prosperous center of culture and trade—platform shoes were worn to keep long skirts from dragging through the city's dirty (and often flooded) streets. In addition to this practical purpose, the elevated shoe became a prominent status symbol in Venetian society for both men and women.

One of the earliest and most extreme types of elevated shoe was the *chopine*, worn in Italy and Spain from the fifteenth to seventeenth centuries. These were mules (backless shoes) with teetering platforms positioned toward the front of the shoe ranging in height from three to six inches, with some surviving examples measuring up to twenty inches tall. They featured fabric uppers (often richly ornamented with metallic lace, tassels, and ribbon trimming) with wood or cork platform soles. Chopines were worn exclusively by women, and—because they were so difficult to walk in—were limited to women of leisure. Noblewomen in those of a more substantial height required the assistance of a pair of lady's maids for balance. Not only did this elevated footwear grant the wearer physical prominence, but it also increased her sartorial reputation. Due to the increased height, additional fabric was needed to ensure that the wearer's feet remained concealed by her skirt. The lengthening of fashionable garments would have been seen as an act of conspicuous consumption at a time when textiles were scarcer, and thus highly valued. Though they were mainly worn by noblewomen, chopines have also become historically associated with well-positioned courtesans—establishing an early connection between the platform shoe and notions of power and sexuality.

The first proper high heel emerged from a technological development in which stacked leather was used to elevate the back of the shoe. By midcentury, heeled shoes became the more common style for upper-class men and women who sought to demonstrate their socioeconomic standing by literally elevating themselves. Examples of this style feature pointed toes—some of which were exaggerated and curled upward. Domed soles and curved heels that flared at the base were other markers of high style toward the end of the century. Fabric uppers were often embellished with elaborate embroidery.

Another variation that prevailed in the second half of the century was the *slap-sole* shoe. While heels afforded men the benefit of being able to secure their feet in stirrups while horse-back riding, they also had the drawback of sinking into the mud upon dismount. Soon, men began adding a flat sole to the bottom of the shoe, which would be attached only at the front. When they walked, there would be a slapping sound when the detached back of the sole struck the heel of the shoe. Women's footwear followed in this style, with the option to have the flat sole firmly attached to the heel.

***Chopines*, 1590–1610.**
Italian. Tooled leather over wood; trimmed with metallic braid.

Chopine, **late 17th–early 18th century.**
Italian. Silk velvet-covered wood with tooled-leather sole;
embellished with gilt-metal lace, silk satin ribbon,
metallic woven trim, metal nails, and tassels.

15

Shoemaker's sample shoes, 1610–20.
Probably Italian. Stamped and punched leather;
trimmed with silk tassels.

***Chopines,* c. 1600.**
Italian. Carved pine wood covered in kid-leather
with punched decoration.

***Mules*, c. 1660.**
Dutch. Embroidered silk upper with leather sole.

***Mule*, 1600–1625.**
British. Silk upper embroidered with metallic thread;
linen lining and leather sole.

Chopines, 1600–1620.
Italian. Carved wood covered with silk velvet;
trimmed with silk ribbon, silver gilt bobbin lace,
and woven silver gilt lace.

Chopine, **1590–1610.**
Italian. Silk velvet trimmed with gold lace,
metallic braid, shirred ribbon, and tassel;
leather lining with incised pattern.

Shoes, **c. 1650.**
British. Silk velvet with leather sole and metallic embroidery.

Slipper, **1675–1710.**
European. Linen upper covered with metallic embroidery;
domed-leather sole with stacked heel.

***Slap-sole shoes,* c. 1670.**
Possibly Italian. Leather upper trimmed with silk satin
featuring straw appliqué; silk laces with decorative tassels;
leather lining and sole.

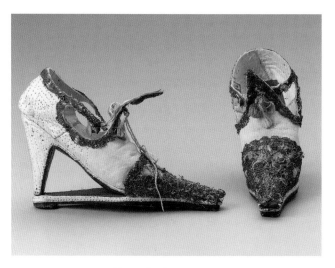

***Slap-sole shoes,* 1660s.**
Italian. Leather upper trimmed with metallic bobbin lace and
silk brocade embroidered with gold and silver metal threads;
silk laces with decorative tassels; leather lining and sole. 25

Shoes, 1690–1700.
French. Leather upper with silk-embroidered floral motifs.

Shoes, **1690–1710.**
European. Leather upper with silk-embroidered floral motifs;
domed-leather sole with white-leather rand.

Latchet shoes, 1690–1720.
Probably Italian. Silk velvet upper embroidered with
metallic yarns; trimmed with metallic fringe and
silk ribbon; leather sole and wood heel.

***Latchet shoe,* late 17th century.**
English. Silk satin upper embellished with metallic lace;
leather sole and covered wood heel.

CHAPTER TWO
18th Century

The prevailing aesthetics of the late Baroque and Rococo periods were strongly influenced by French tastes, which were pervasive across Europe throughout the eighteenth century. Though feet remained hidden beneath wide skirts for most of this period, footwear continued to be highly decorative. Soles were made of leather, while boldly patterned, brocaded, or embroidered silks were favored for fabric uppers. It was not unusual for an upper-class woman to have the textile of a pair of shoes made to match a dress. Silk shoes consisted of two side-seam openings and *latchets* (side straps) that overlapped across the vamp (top of the shoe). In the early decades of the century, fabric ties were used to secure the closure, but these were later replaced by metal buckles that often featured cut-paste stones or real jewels. Latchets widened as the attached decorative buckles grew in size around the 1770s, when skirts were shortened to the ankle and women's shoes were revealed.

Different methods of decoration prevailed, but the most common design feature from about 1690 to 1750 was a wide strip of metallic braid that ran up the center of the vamp. Metallic cord and bullion lace were other fashionable methods of adornment. In some examples, rows of braid cover the entire fabric upper, while in others, elaborate rows of flame stitching create an eye-catching zigzag pattern. By the last quarter of the eighteenth century, embroidery patterns for shoe vamps were published in women's magazines, which allowed fabric uppers to be embroidered at home and then brought to a shoemaker. Up until the 1760s, a white *rand* (thin strip of leather along the front edge of the sole) was a conspicuous feature of high-quality footwear. In order to protect silk shoes from the dirt of outdoor wear, matching *clogs* (also called *pattens* or *overshoes*) could be worn. These had a reinforced leather sole and midstep support, which made it easier to walk on cobblestone or uneven roads. Mules remained a popular indoor style for women, with heeled variations for the boudoir.

British-made shoes tended to have a lower, stockier heel, while the French preferred a higher, thinner one. One particular French style called the "Pompadour" featured a heel placed further underneath the instep, causing the foot to appear smaller and daintier. The fashionable heel shape of the period was curved at the waist with a flared base, and was deemed the "Louis heel" for France's King Louis XV. However, it was his predecessor Louis XIV, the Sun King, who is credited with establishing the fashion for high heels in the previous century.

Under Louis XIV's edict, the *talon rouge* (red heel) became the ultimate mark of royal distinction. The painted red heel signified members of the French court into the eighteenth century and was inherited as a status symbol by aristocrats in other countries as well. The onset of the French Revolution in 1789 not only put an end to the talon rouge, but diminished the fashion for the high heel altogether—which was perceived as a symbol of the corrupt aristocracy. The revolution led to changing styles and sensibilities in all aspects of art and design; as a result, women's shoes in the 1790s became simple and slipper-like, with a very low heel.

Shoe with matching patten, **1720–30.**
English. Silk damask trimmed with
silver metallic braid; leather sole.

Shoes with matching pattens, 1740–49.
English. Silk brocade with leather sole and linen lining.

***Mules*, early 18th century.**
European. Silk and linen upper with Florentine embroidery;
leather sole.

***Tie shoe*, c. 1720.**
English. Brocaded silk upper with leather sole.

***Tie shoes*, early 18th century.**
French. Punched-leather upper; silk cord ties with decorative
tassels; painted stacked-leather heel.

***Mules*, late 17th–early 18th century.**
European. Silk velvet upper trimmed with ruched silk tape and
silver pointed toe piece; leather-covered Louis heel.

Latchet shoes, 1700–1715.
English. Silk satin upper embellished
with silver lace and metal sequins;
leather sole.

Buckle shoe, 1700–1729.
Probably British. Silk upper embellished
with metallic lace and rows of braid;
metal buckle with cut-paste stones; leather sole.

Latchet shoe, **1720–49.**
Probably British. Embroidered silk upper with leather sole
and white-leather rand.

***Latchet shoes*, 1700–1729.**
British. Linen upper with wool flame stitch embroidery,
embellished with metallic braid; leather sole and
white-leather rand.

43

Latchet shoes, 1732–59.
British. Patterned silk velvet upper with metallic ribbon trim;
leather sole with white-leather rand and red Louis heel.

Latchet shoes, 1750–69.
British. Linen upper with wool flame stitch embroidery;
Louis heel covered with printed silk; leather sole and
white-leather rand.

45

***Tie shoe,* 1720–30.**
British. Silk brocade upper with red Louis heel;
leather sole and white-leather rand.

Pompadour shoes, 1750s–60s.
French. Brocaded silk upper with silk damask-covered heel;
latchets fastened with jeweled buckle; domed-leather sole.

Latchet shoes, 1730–55.
Probably British. Silk upper embellished with metallic braid;
leather sole with white-leather rand.

Buckle shoes, **1720–39.**
European. Silk upper with metallic gold embroidery
and covered Louis heel; latchets fastened with
jeweled buckle; leather sole.

49

Latchet shoes, 1710–49.
British. Silk upper with metallic gold embroidery and
covered Louis heel; leather sole.

Latchet shoes with turn-down tongue, 1750s–60s.
European. Silk satin upper with metallic embroidery and
covered Louis heel; domed-leather sole.

***Buckle shoes,* 1750s.**
British. Silk upper embellished with silver lace and metallic
braid; latchets fastened with jeweled buckle; covered
Louis heel and leather sole.

Tie shoes, **1725–50.**
English. Silk taffeta upper with floral embroidery;
linen lining and leather sole.

Latchet shoes, c. 1770.
English, worn in America. Patterned silk upper with covered
Louis heel; linen lining and leather sole.

Latchet shoe, 1760–80.
British. Patterned silk upper and covered Louis heel trimmed
with metallic braid; leather sole.

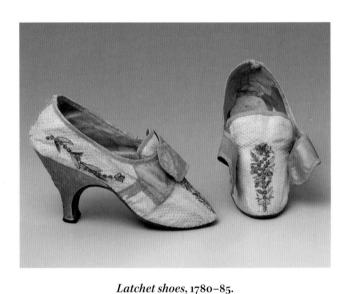

Latchet shoes, 1780–85.
European. Figured silk embroidered with metallic yarns
and spangles; silk satin latchets and covered heel;
linen lining and leather sole.

Buckle shoes, 1770s–80s.
American or European. Embroidered silk upper and
covered Louis heel; latchets fastened with
cast-metal buckle; leather sole.

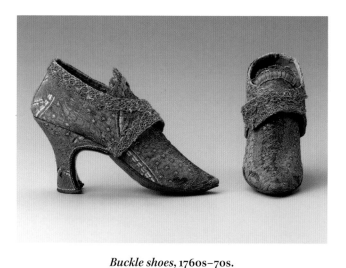

Buckle shoes, **1760s–70s.**
European (possibly Italian). Figured silk upper with gilt-silver
brocading and covered Louis heel; metallic lace and braid
trimming; leather lining and sole.

***Slippers,* 1780–90.**
Possibly French. Silk upper embellished with gilt-metal coiled
fringe, silver sequins, and painted paper appliqué; cotton lining
with drawstring; leather sole and covered Louis heel.

Slippers, 1780–89.
European. Silk satin upper with fringe trimming; leather sole.

Slippers, 1780–1800.
British. Kid-leather upper with stenciled design, bound
with ribbed silk tape and embellished with a pom-pom;
leather sole and covered heel.

***Slippers,* 1790s.**
British. Dyed-leather upper with silk ribbon ties;
leather sole.

Buckle shoes with Italian heel, **1797.**
British. Silk satin upper with silver-thread embroidery, sequins,
and small glass-paste ovals; latchets fastened with metal
buckle; covered Italian heel and leather sole.

CHAPTER THREE
Early 19th Century • 1800–1850

Women's fashion during the first half of the nineteenth century saw simplification in accordance with Neoclassical tastes, before gradually blossoming into the softer styles of the Romantic period. This era is marked by a dramatic evolution in the fashionable silhouette—from the narrow, empire-waisted dresses of the 1810s, to the voluminous gigot sleeves of the 1830s, and the dome-shaped crinoline skirts of the 1850s. Yet, interestingly, the design of footwear remains fairly consistent throughout.

In a departure from the French aristocracy of the eighteenth century, Empress Joséphine Bonaparte wore flat slippers to her coronation in 1804. While her choice of footwear may have been politically motivated, it set the fashion standard, and women's shoes remained flat until the 1860s. Strict codes of dress were established in the nineteenth century that required women to wear different ensembles for different times of day. As a result, shoes were designated for daytime or evening wear. House slippers and daywear shoes were typically more colorful and ornate, while plain silk satin slippers with ribbon ties were favored for the evening. In the first two decades of the nineteenth century, a sharply pointed toe was fashionable, and slippers featured cotton uppers with contrasting embroidered leather tips. Very short heels were seen in the first few years of the century, but shoes were completely flat by the 1810s. While the overall shape of fashionable slippers remained slender and tight, a square toe became more popular around 1840. This slightly wider vamp allowed for decoration like embroidery or horizontal ribbon stripes. Though designs were relatively simplistic during this era, what little adornment there was focused on the toe area, which might peek out from beneath the hem of a long skirt. The fashion for square-toed slippers also coincided with the introduction of pointe work in ballet—made popular by famed dancer Marie Taglioni.

As hemlines rose in the 1830s, ankle boots became the standard daytime footwear and remained fashionable through the 1860s. Side lace-up closures allowed the soft fabric uppers to fit closely to the ankle, which was meant to look as dainty as possible. One variation, called the *gaiter boot*, used contrasting materials to imitate the appearance of slippers worn with gaiters (lower leg coverings). Because the delicate boots of the early nineteenth century had such thin leather soles, pattens or overshoes could be worn over them for outdoor wear. These were considered a utilitarian accessory; yet, examples of boots and pattens designed to match do survive.

Some technological developments advanced fabrication during this period. In 1837, the elastic side boot was patented and an early example was presented to the young Queen Victoria. This allowed boots to be more easily slipped on, though side-laced and buttoned boots would remain in fashion for the rest of the century. An important evolution in footwear production during this period was the designation between right and left shoes. Previously, they had been made identically as *straights*—which streamlined construction, but proved to be uncomfortable.

Slippers, **1805–10.**
European. Cotton upper with contrasting leather tip
and fringed ornament.

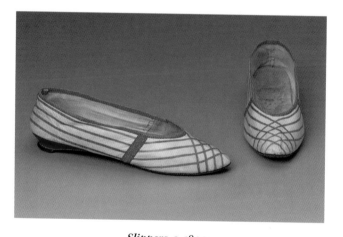

Slippers, c. 1800.
John Staton, English, active about 1800. Painted kid-leather
upper with silk ribbon trimming and linen lining.

Lace-up shoes with pattens, 1810–30.
French. Silk upper with cotton lining and silk ribbon laces;
pattens with reinforced leather sole.

Lace-up shoes, **1805–10.**
French or English, worn in America. Cotton upper with
contrasting leather decorated with silk chain-stitch
embroidery; silk ribbon laces, linen lining, and leather sole.

Slippers, **c. 1810.**
American. Silk satin uppers decorated with metallic
embroidery, spangles, and a silk ribbon bow.

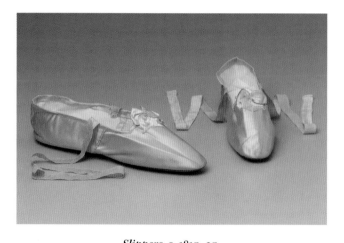

***Slippers*, c. 1815–25.**
Probably French, worn in America. Silk satin upper with silk
ribbon laces, linen lining, and leather sole.

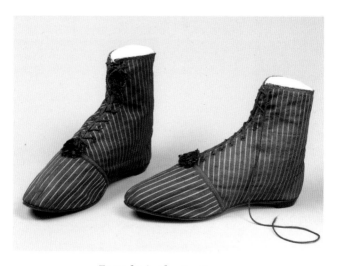

Front-lacing boots, 1812–20.
British. Striped cotton upper with leather sole,
decorated with silk rosette.

Front-lacing boots, **1818.**
Italian. Silk satin upper with fringed trimming,
woven silk laces, linen lining, and leather sole.

Lace-up shoes, **1810–29.**
Probably British. Silk upper with ribbon ties
and leather sole.

***Slippers,* 1810–20.**
American. Quilted silk upper with silk ribbon tie
and leather sole.

Moccasin-inspired slippers, c. 1825.
British. Silk satin upper with wool embroidery
and leather sole.

Ankle boots and matching pattens, 1825–30.
American. Kid-leather upper with reinforced leather sole.

Gaiter boots, **c. 1835.**
French. Cotton upper with leather toe and leather sole.

Evening slippers, 1815–20.
Vandervell, British. Patterned silk upper with ribbon
decoration and leather sole.

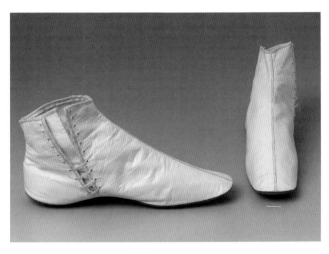

Ankle boots, **1825–50.**
American. Kid-leather upper with ribbon laces,
cotton lining, and leather sole.

Gaiter boots, c. 1838.
Probably American. Silk satin and leather upper
with ribbon laces, linen lining, and leather sole.

House slippers, 1835–45.
French. Embroidered silk upper with leather sole.

Slippers, **1830–50.**
French. Uppers of strung glass beads (sablé) with metallic braid
trimming, silk lining, and leather sole.

Evening slippers, 1830–35.
British. Silk satin upper with bow;
kid-leather lining and sole.

Evening slippers, **1835–45.**
Probably American. Silk satin upper
with ribbon laces; leather sole.

Slippers, **1815–25.**
French, worn in America. Leather upper, silk ribbon;
linen lining with cord drawstring.

Slippers, c. 1840.
French. Leather upper with silk embroidery and
silk ribbon laces; leather lining and sole.

89

***Evening slippers,* 1840–49.**
Gundry & Sons, French. Silk satin upper with metallic ribbon
stripes and rosette embellishment; leather sole.

Wedding slippers, 1835–45.
Probably French. Silk satin upper adorned with ribbon
and lace; leather sole.

***Slippers**, 1849.*
American. Embroidered silk satin upper with
ribbon trimming and leather sole.

***Slippers,* 1845–60.**
Probably French. Striped cotton upper with
silk bow and leather sole.

Slippers, **mid-1800s.**
American. Glazed-leather upper decorated
with silk appliqué and chain-stitch embroidery; leather sole.

***Slippers*, 1840s.**
Russian, worn in America. Silk velvet upper
decorated with silk embroidery and ribbon work;
ermine-fur trimming and leather sole.

CHAPTER FOUR
Late 19th Century · 1850–1900

ashion thrived during this period, and one thing was consistent across Belle Epoque Paris, Victorian England, and Gilded Age America—a taste for sumptuous excess. Though they evolved dramatically in shape during the second half of the nineteenth century, skirts consistently skimmed the floor and concealed footwear beneath. Still, shoe design followed in the styles of fashionable dress and became increasingly ornate. Heeled shoes came back into style by the 1870s, and the curved, waisted heels of footwear mimicked the corseted, hourglass-shaped bodices of Victorian-era dress. As heels grew taller, they altered the wearer's posture by tilting the chest forward and the hips backward—further accentuating the posterior fullness of the bustle gowns that defined fashion in the 1870s and 1880s.

Time-of-day dress codes remained rigidly in place for upper-class women, and elaborate Gilded Age dress practices deemed different shoes necessary to complete each ensemble. In the last quarter of the century, the wealthiest American women were known to make annual trips to Paris to purchase clothing for the season from the most notable couturiers. There, they also patronized renowned shoemakers like L. Perchellet to create custom footwear to coordinate with specific couture gowns. For less moneyed women, matching evening shoes were more easily attainable by dyeing white silk satin slippers. The first synthetic aniline dye was discovered in 1856—a brilliant shade of purple called *mauveine*. Other vibrant colors followed, which quickly dominated fashion and footwear.

Boots remained standard for daytime wear, and *high-button boots* that extended above the ankle were the go-to choice for activity outside of the home. The numerous button closures could be fastidiously fastened with the aid of a button hook, and lace-up versions later became available. Although these boots were rather modest in appearance, the sight of them was considered quite scandalous—which led them to be eroticized by the turn of the century. Daytime slippers were also considered quite intimate and were meant for wearing around the house or receiving close friends.

For evening wear, the flat slippers of the 1850s and 1860s were commonly embellished with large fabric rosettes or embroidery on the vamp. Heels returned to fashion in the decade that followed, adorned with beading and ribbon work. A less common—though highly fashionable—evening style emerged in France around 1880, which featured a high back with wide ribbons that would be tied around the ankle to make large bows. In the 1890s, solid-colored silk satin *pumps* (strapless heeled shoes with a closed toe) were typical, though there were slight variations in proportion across different countries. The French style featured short and tight vamps, with a distinctive upcurve of the sole, while the American style exhibited a longer vamp with less curve in the pointed toe. Evening boots emerged in the last quarter of the nineteenth century, which were made of silk satin with elaborately embroidered vamps. To protect delicate silk evening shoes en route to a formal event, overshoes called *carriage boots* could be worn.

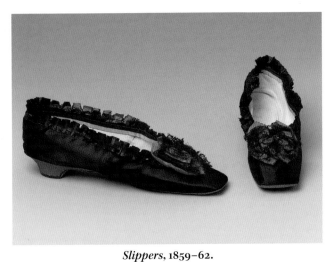

Slippers, 1859–62.
French. Silk satin upper trimmed with lace and pleated satin
ribbon; contrast taffeta bow and covered heel; leather sole.

Evening boots, 1840–65.
British. Embroidered silk satin upper with contrast satin-
covered heel; leather sole.

***Boots*, c. 1850.**
English. Silk satin upper with cotton lining and leather sole.

Boots, 1865.
French. Silk satin upper with linen lining and leather sole.

Slippers, c. 1860.
American or European. Cashmere wool upper
with silk embroidery and leather sole.

***Slippers*, c. 1866.**
De Haven, American. Silk velvet upper
with silk embroidery and leather sole.

Boudoir slippers, 1870–75.
American. Velvet and quilted silk upper with
taffeta adornment and jeweled buckle.

Pump, **1873.**
French. Silk satin upper adorned with metallic embroidery,
fringe trimming, and silk braid.

Evening slipper, 1860–70.
British. Silk satin upper with ribbon stripes and rosettes.

***Slippers*, c. 1870.**
Julien Mayer, French. Cotton upper with pleated
silk trimming and metal buckle.

***Slipper,* c. 1850–70.**
French. Silk velvet upper embellished with
gilt-silver embroidery and seed pearls;
silk satin lining and leather sole.

***Boudoir slippers*, 1865–85.**
E.D. Burt & Co. Fine Shoes, American. Quilted silk upper
with velvet trimming and jeweled buckle;
covered heel and leather sole.

Evening slippers, 1880.
J. Ferry, French. Patterned silk upper with leather sole;
made to match couture evening dress.

Pumps with instep strap, 1880–85.
American. Leather upper adorned
with silk satin and glass beads.

Evening shoes, 1875–85.
French. Silk satin upper embellished with glass beads;
wide-ribbon ankle ties and leather sole.

Evening shoes, 1875–85.
French. Silk satin upper with ribbon-work embroidery;
wide-ribbon ankle ties and leather sole.

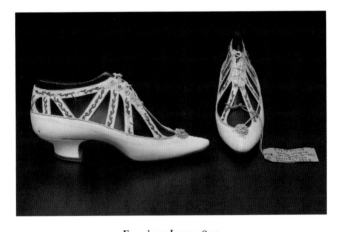

Evening shoes, 1893.
American. Suede upper with open cutwork embellished
with cut brass beads and silk ribbon rosettes;
silk cord laces and leather sole.

Evening shoes, c. 1895.
L. Perchellet, French. Silk satin upper with metallic embroidery;
shaped instep strap and leather sole.

Evening pumps, 1895.
L. Perchellet, French. Silk satin upper embellished with glass
beads and metal sequins; made to match evening gown.

Evening pumps, 1885–90.
J. Ferry, French. Panné silk velvet upper with decorative bow.

High-button boots, 1870–90.
American. Kid-leather upper with scalloped edge and button
closure; silk lining, linen interlining, and leather sole.

***Evening oxfords*, c. 1891.**
Alfred J. Cammeyer, American, active 1875–1930s.
Metallic kid-leather with ribbon laces.

High-button boots, 1875–80.
French. Silk velvet upper with scalloped edge and button
closure; silk faille lining and leather sole.

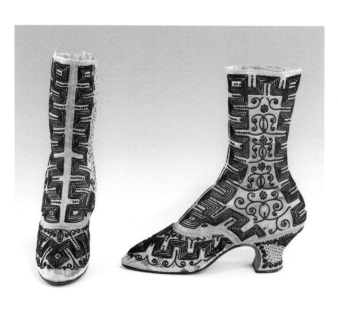

Evening boots, 1885–90.
Probably French. Silk satin upper with
metallic embroidery; leather sole.

Evening boots, 1865–75.
British. Ribbed-silk upper trimmed with bobbin lace and
ribbon; silk-covered heel and leather sole.

Evening boots, 1870s.
French or British. Silk satin upper with multiple latchets for
lace-up ladder effect; silk bow and cord lacing.

***Boudoir slippers*, c. 1890.**
American or European. Quilted silk upper with
fur trimming and leather sole.

Boudoir slippers, c. 1892.
Rosenbloom's, American. Kid-leather upper
with decorative tassels.

High-button boots, 1895–1915.
Anton Capek, British. Leather upper with glacé finish,
scalloped edge, button closure, and Louis heel.

High-button boots, c. 1895.
W. Coulson, British. Leather upper with scalloped edge,
button closure, and eroticized Louis heel.

CHAPTER FIVE
Early 20th Century · 1900–1935

The first three decades of the twentieth century marked a period of dramatic social change for women—a journey that can be effectively chronicled through footwear. From the rigid formalities of the Edwardian era to the heightened exuberance of the Roaring Twenties, fashion evolved to reflect the female experience. The rise and fall of hemlines during this period had a profound impact on footwear design—resulting in flashier embellishments and style lines intended to elongate newly exposed legs.

The early years of the period predominantly followed the styles and sensibilities of the late nineteenth century, where modest high-button boots reigned during the day and classic silk pumps were worn in the evening. Specialty shoes for sporting and bathing were also part of the Edwardian lady's wardrobe. Soon, lace-up oxfords and pumps with *Mary Jane* style straps across the instep entered the footwear repertoire, and eventually became mainstays in twentieth-century shoe design. Sturdy leather oxfords and ankle boots became the emblem of the working woman, as well as the suffragist—who marched in the streets for the first two decades of the century, demanding her right to vote.

Pumps with multiple crossover button closures were especially fashionable during the 1910s. Aside from World War I, the defining aspect of this period was the birth of modern dress—which effectively eliminated the corset from women's fashion. Avant-garde modernists like Paul Poiret drew upon Eastern influences to create styles that liberated the female form, and Orientalist footwear was created by the likes of Pietro Yantorny—the self-proclaimed "most expensive shoemaker in the world." Another notable shoemaker who gained prominence during this period was André Perugia, who collaborated with many of Paris's top couturiers, including Poiret.

Dance crazes from this era naturally affected footwear design and even became the catalysts for fashion trends. As the Tango Craze seized Europe in the 1910s, *tango shoes* and *tango boots* became popular both on and off the dance floor. These styles featured crossing laces that extended all the way up the ankle from the top of the vamp, to ensure that they were securely fastened for dancing. Tango shoes also tended to be quite flashy, in order to draw the eye to the dancer's complex footwork.

A similar tactic was employed in designing Jazz Age footwear, when the Charleston gained widespread popularity in the 1920s. Eye-catching *T-strap* evening shoes—with closed toes, closed backs, and open quarters—were on full display due to shortened hemlines and were extraordinary in their glittering extravagance. Metallic leathers like gilded kid became more prevalent in footwear, and even luxurious fabric uppers were further embellished with glass beads, rhinestones, sequins, and jeweled buckles. Decorative interchangeable heels bore the hallmarks of the Art Deco aesthetic prevalent in architecture in the late 1920s and early 1930s. These were typically made of wood with a celluloid overlay and fabricated to emulate tortoiseshell, lacquer, and mother-of-pearl. Ostentatious geometric patterns rendered in paint and inlaid rhinestones provided another layer of embellishment. These detachable heels added a touch of glamour to any shoe, but they have since become valued as art objects in themselves.

Dinner oxford, 1900–1910.
Charles Strohbeck, Inc., American. Leather upper with glacé
finish, embellished with glass beads.

***Lace-up boots*, c. 1915.**
English. Brown glacé kid-leather upper and black calf-leather
vamp with Cuban heel.

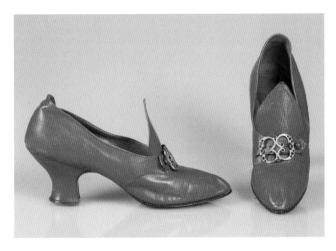

***Pumps*, c. 1910.**
J. & J. Slater, American. Leather upper with metal
and rhinestone buckle.

Fetish boots, 1900–1920.
Maniatis Bottier, Paris, French. Leather upper with
contrast vamp and scalloped button closure.

***Evening shoe**, 1914–19.*
Designed by Pietro Yantorny, Italian, 1874–1936. Silk upper with
lace appliqué and metal buckle with inlaid jet.

Evening shoes, c. 1908.
Jack Jacobus Ltd., British. Kid-leather upper with glacé finish,
embellished with jet beading.

Tango boots, c. 1918.
Bray Bros., American. Gilt-leather upper with crossing laces.

***Tango shoes*, 1914.**
Peter Robinson Ltd., British. Brocaded silk satin with silver lamé
ribbon ties and gilt-paste studded eyelets.

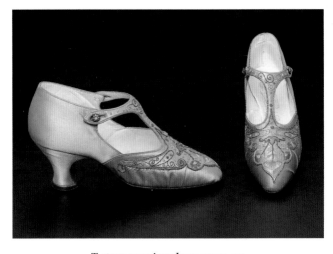

T-strap evening shoes, 1920–30.
French. Silk satin upper with metallic embroidery
and glass-stone buttons.

Evening shoes, **1910–25.**
Jones, Peterson & Newhall Co., American, founded 1903.
Kid-leather upper with beaded embroidery
and satin-ribbon ankle strap.

143

***Shoes*, c. 1925.**
British. Leather upper with elastic gussets and
openwork instep embellished with steel beads.

Evening shoes, 1910–20.
Sorosis, American. Gilt-leather upper embellished
with glass beads and rhinestones.

Evening slippers, 1930–32.
Designed by André Perugia, French, 1893–1977. Kid-leather
upper with metallic gold pigment.

***Mules*, 1914–19.**
Designed by Pietro Yantorny, Italian, 1874–1936.
Silk upper with metallic embroidery.

Evening shoes, c. 1925.
F. Pinet, Paris, French, founded 1855. Silk satin upper
with floral silk embroidery.

Evening shoes, 1915–20.
Alfred J. Cammeyer, American, active 1875–1930s.
Leather upper embellished with glass beads.

T-strap evening shoes, c. 1924.
Probably American. Patterned silk upper with
metallic threads and T-strap fastening.

***Le Bal* evening slippers, 1924.**
Designed by André Perugia, French, 1893–1977, and Paul Poiret,
French, 1879–1944. Silk and leather upper embellished with
glass beads depicting Paul and his wife Denise.

T-strap shoes, c. 1921.
British. Leather and lizard-skin upper with T-strap fastening.

***T-strap shoes*, 1925.**
Ducerf, Scavini & Fils, French. Leather upper with wood
and celluloid, compression molded.

Day shoes, **c. 1930.**
French. Striped cotton upper with
covered wood heel and leather sole.

***Day shoes*, c. 1927.**
French. Calf-leather upper with stamped and painted design.

Evening shoes, c. 1925.
Nancy Haggerty Shoes, Inc., American. Silk satin upper with
covered wood heel, rhinestone buckle, and leather sole.

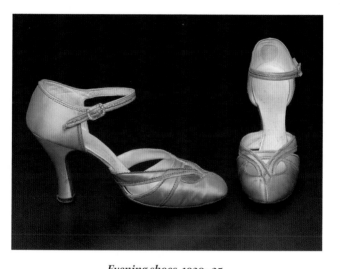

Evening shoes, 1930–35.
J. & J. Slater, American. Silk satin upper trimmed with metallic
leather; rhinestone buckle and leather sole.

T-strap evening shoes, c. 1925.
Bob, Inc., N.Y., American. Metallic-leather upper
with painted design and T-strap fastening.

T-strap evening shoes, 1934.
Manufactured by Fenton Footwear, American, for
Saks Fifth Avenue, American, founded 1924. Silk satin upper
trimmed with metallic leather; T-strap fastening.

Oxford pumps, c. 1930.
Thayer McNeil Co., American. Silk upper with woven-metallic thread; silk ribbon laces and rhinestone eyelets.

Evening sandals, 1928–29.
Designed by André Perugia, French, 1893–1977. Gilt-leather
upper with cast-metal heel.

T-strap evening shoes, **c. 1927.**
Marshall Field & Company, American, founded 1881.
Pearlized-leather upper with pavé rhinestones
and T-strap fastening.

***Day shoes,* c. 1925.**
British. Leather upper with interlaced decorative panel
and stained pearl buttons.

T-strap evening shoes, c. 1934.
American. Silk satin upper with metallic-leather
T-strap fastening.

Evening shoes, **c. 1933.**
Saks & Company, American. Brocaded-silk upper with
metallic-leather strap and heel.

165

T-strap evening shoe, 1933.
Seymour Troy Originals, American. Rhinestone-encrusted
upper with leather sole.

Evening shoe, 1935.
Delman, American, founded 1919. Silk satin and metallic-leather
latticework upper embellished with multicolored rhinestones.

CHAPTER SIX
Mid-20th Century • 1935–1965

S hoe design in the mid-twentieth century mirrored the
changing global landscape—from Depression-era escapism
to modern innovation, from wartime utility to postwar femininity. Prominent footwear designers emerged in France and Italy,
some of whom were hired by savvy American manufacturers
like Herman Delman, who partnered with department stores
such as Saks and Bergdorf Goodman to increase distribution.

The 1930s and 1940s were largely defined by the Great
Depression and World War II. During these global crises, access
to clothing was severely diminished—which led to accessories
becoming a focal point in fashionable dressing. In Europe, wartime rationing restricted the use of leather and rubber in civil-
ian footwear production. However, from these limitations came
ingenuity, as shoemakers in German-occupied France resorted
to inventive uses of cork, wood, straw, and cellophane—eventually leading to new trends in fashion. For example, the
constraint of only being allowed to purchase a single pair of
shoes in a year gave makers the impetus to create thick soles,
which took longer to wear down. Despite being born out of

necessity, the platform shoes gained popularity in fashionable footwear. They would eventually evolve into a split-sole design—with a separate wedge heel and elevated foresole—often paired with a peep-toe cutout and an ankle strap during the 1940s.

One designer known for his creative use of unconventional materials was Salvatore Ferragamo. With his impressive roster of star clientele, he brought international attention to the fine art of Italian shoemaking. He is credited with introducing the cork wedge in the late 1930s, the most famous example being the Rainbow sandal, designed for Judy Garland. He consistently experimented with form, often approaching shoe design in a way that was distinctly conceptual. His signature F-heel was a stylized, undercut wedge that suggested cantilever support. It formed the base of his Invisible Sandal, which utilized nylon monofilament to create a barely there upper. Another Ferragamo innovation was the *shank*—a metal support for the arch of the foot, which helped take weight off the heel and toe.

Postwar fashion was defined by Dior's New Look, which exuded femininity and ushered in the Golden Age of Couture. During this period, the House of Dior began a legendary collaboration with celebrated shoe designer Roger Vivier, who had previously designed for renowned brands such as Bally, Rayne, and Delman. Vivier created luxuriously embellished pieces under the Dior label from 1953 to 1963, marking the first and only time the famed couturier partnered with a designer for footwear. It was during the early 1950s that the *stiletto* was born, with Vivier, Ferragamo, and Perugia all being credited with its invention. This style—which translates to "dagger" or "knife" in Italian—is notable for its ultraskinny heel, made possible by the support of a steel rod. One Vivier variation was the Choc heel, which was introduced in 1959 and had a distinctive concave curve. He continued to experiment with heel shapes into the 1960s—creating the Virgule (or "Comma") heel that curved inward, and the New Style heel that repositioned the short *kitten* heel at a slanted angle underneath the instep.

Perhaps the most imaginative designer to emerge from this era was New York–based Beth Levine, who started designing for a label named for her husband (Herbert Levine) in 1949. She created such whimsical innovations as the Spring-o-lator—an elasticated insole that helped high-heeled mules securely hug the arch of the foot. Another, the topless No-Shoe, attached to the foot via adhesive pads and boasted an uninterrupted leg line due to the absent upper.

Evening pumps, **1935–49.**
French. Leather upper with painted design and cutouts.

***Cutout wedge sandals*, late 1940s.**
Saks Fifth Avenue, American, founded 1924, after a design
by André Perugia, French, 1893–1977. Gold-painted leather
with red-leather lining.

173

Rainbow sandals, 1938.
Designed by Salvatore Ferragamo, Italian, 1898–1960.
Gold-leather upper with cork heel covered
with multicolored suede.

Platform sandals, **c. 1940.**
Victor, American. Suede upper and undercut wedge heel.

***Platform sandals*, c. 1940.**
Saks Fifth Avenue, American, founded 1924.
Printed-silk upper and plant-fiber sole.

***Evening platform sandals,* 1938.**
Designed by Salvatore Ferragamo, Italian, 1898–1960.
Leather and silk upper; platform sole embellished
with rhinestones.

177

***Ankle boots*, Winter 1939–40.**
Designed by Elsa Schiaparelli, French (born Italy), 1890–1973.
Leopard-skin upper with mother-of-pearl
buttons and leather sole.

Peep-toe pumps, **1937–39.**
Delman, American, founded 1919.
Leather upper and covered heel.

***Sandals*, c. 1943.**
Delman, American, founded 1919. Knitted-straw upper
with cork heels, cotton ties, and shell embellishments.

Sandals, c. 1950.
Bonwit Teller & Co., American, founded 1907.
Straw-braid upper and leather sole.

***Platform sandals**, c. 1943.*
Penét Shoes, Inc., American. Suede upper;
suede-covered platform and heel.

Platform peep-toe sandals, 1940s.
American. White-suede upper;
brown leather-covered platform and heel.

Platform peep-toe sandals, 1946–49.
Henri, American. Multicolored-leather upper; leather-covered
platform and heel.

Platform peep-toe shoes, **c. 1950.**
Mackay Starr, American. Silk upper with rhinestone buckle;
gilt-leather platform and insole.

Invisible Sandal with undercut wedge heel (F-heel), **1947.**
Designed by Salvatore Ferragamo, Italian, 1898–1960. Metallic-
leather wedge with nylon-monofilament upper.

***Shoe with undercut wedge (F-heel)*, 1948–50.**
Designed by Salvatore Ferragamo, Italian, 1898–1960. Purple
suede trimmed with gold-metallic kid-leather.

Shoes, **c. 1950.**
Seymour Troy Originals, American. Leather.

Stiletto pumps, **1956.**
Designed by Beth Levine, American, 1914–2006, designed for
Herbert Levine Inc., American, founded 1949.
Suede upper with silk-net embellishment.

***Sandals*, c. 1949.**
Delman, American, founded 1919. Multicolored suede.

***Mule*, 1954.**
Designed by Roger Vivier, French, 1907–1998, for House of Dior,
French, founded 1946. Silk satin upper and covered heel
with feathered adornment.

Stiletto pumps, 1955.
Designed by Roger Vivier, French, 1907–1998,
for House of Dior, French, founded 1946. Silk satin upper
with silk and metallic embroidery; leather sole.

Evening stiletto pumps, **1957.**
Designed by Roger Vivier, French, 1907–1998,
for House of Dior, French, founded 1946. Embroidered silk satin
upper with rhinestone-embellished rosettes.

Platform wedge sandal, **late 1940s.**
Manufactured by Fenton Footwear, American, for Saks Fifth
Avenue, American, founded 1924. Suede upper and covered
platform embellished with brass studs.

Pump, c. 1950.
Designed by André Perugia, French, 1893–1977.
Suede upper and metal heel.

Spring-o-lator mules, 1955–61.
Probably American. Silk satin upper with
rhinestone-embellished rosette, Spring-o-lator
elastic bridge, and metal heel.

Evening sandals, 1958.
Designed by Roger Vivier, French, 1907–1998,
for House of Dior, French, founded 1946.
Silk satin upper with rosettes.

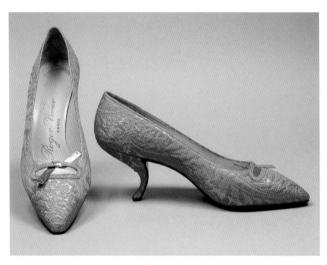

Evening shoes with Virgule ("Comma") heels, **1957.**
Designed by Roger Vivier, French, 1907–1998, for House of Dior,
French, founded 1946. Silk and metallic-thread matelassé
upper and covered heel with patent leather trimming.

Evening shoes with New Style heel, c. 1962.
Designed by Roger Vivier, French, 1907–1998, for House of
Dior, French, founded 1946. Silk satin upper and covered heel,
embellished with glass beads and metallic strips.

Evening shoe with Choc heel, 1960.
Designed by Roger Vivier, French, 1907–1998, for House of Dior,
French, founded 1946. Silk upper covered with feathers.

***Evening boot*, 1957.**
Designed by Roger Vivier, French, 1907–1998, for House of
Dior, French, founded 1946. Silk satin and Chantilly-lace upper
embellished with glass beads and plastic sequins. 201

***Stiletto pumps,* 1960s.**
Saks Fifth Avenue, American, founded 1924. Silk satin upper
embellished with rhinestones.

***Evening boots,* c. 1962.**
Designed by Beth Levine, American, 1914–2006, for Herbert
Levine Inc., American, founded 1949. Silk upper
embellished with metal and rhinestones.

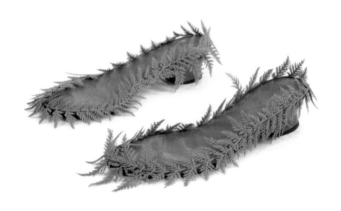

Topless shoes, 1955–60.
Designed by Beth Levine, American, 1914–2006,
for Herbert Levine Inc., American, founded 1949.
Leather and plastic sole; secured with adhesive.

***Mule*, 1962.**
Designed by Beth Levine, American, 1914–2006,
for Herbert Levine Inc., American, founded 1949.
Silk velvet upper with silver-leather sole and rolled heel.

CHAPTER SEVEN
Late 20th Century • 1965–2000

The final decades of the twentieth century were transformed by postmodernism, yielding an eclectic mix of designs which explored futurism, novelty, and revivalism. This era also gave rise to second-wave feminism, and the miniskirt quickly became an emblem of women's liberation. The shortened skirts brought renewed focus to the legs and feet, especially with the introduction of brightly colored and patterned pantyhose. Trousers for women became gradually normalized, notably in boot-cut and bell-bottom styles that were designed to accommodate fashionable footwear.

The mid-1960s saw a proliferation of novelty shoe designs which experimented with synthetic materials like plastics, vinyl, and spandex. Shoes were both clear and colorful, often infused with a sense of wit or whimsy. With the arrival of the Youthquake in 1965, flat or low-heeled Mary Jane styles that resembled children's shoes became popular. For the slightly maturer woman, Roger Vivier designed an elegant alternative that would become one of his best-known styles. The so-called Belle Vivier had a low block heel, a square toe, and a large decorative buckle atop the short vamp. The style was immortalized on-screen by Catherine Deneuve in the 1967 film *Belle de Jour* and has remained a classic staple ever since.

Boots returned to fashion footwear after almost fifty years of absence. The Space Age aesthetic was pioneered by designers like André Courrèges, whose futuristic ensembles were frequently paired with his signature flat white-leather boots. These would eventually give rise to the go-go boot, usually made of patent leather with a chunky heel. However, it is Beth Levine who is credited with reigniting the trend for boots during this period, even designing those famously worn by Nancy Sinatra for the promotion of her 1966 hit song, "These Boots Are Made for Walkin'". Levine experimented with different synthetic materials to create fitted pull-on boots and stocking boots, which extended up over the knee. Her continued creativity and innovation throughout the second half of the century eventually earned her the title of "First Lady of Shoe Design."

Fashion during the 1970s experienced revivals of styles from earlier decades. High-cut leather lace-up boots recalled those worn during the Victorian and Edwardian eras, which sometimes incorporated embroidery made fashionable by the renewed interest in "folk" style. Split-sole platform sandals fabricated from cork and wood evoked those worn by women during World War II. Exaggerated platform shoes became fashionable for both men and women at the onset of the Peacock

Revolution, which challenged gender norms and reintroduced heeled shoes to menswear for the first time in centuries. Platform pumps would eventually reach new heights in the 1990s, when Vivienne Westwood collaborated with Patrick Cox to create sky-high shoes that infamously caused supermodel Naomi Campbell to stumble on the runway.

Pumps were especially fashionable in the 1980s, and reflected the ostentatious tastes of the period. Vivid colors and jeweled embellishments were the hallmark of New York–based shoe company Susan Bennis/Warren Edwards, which became known for its outrageous designs. In an era obsessed with status, designer labels were especially coveted. Perhaps the most desirable shoes by the 1990s were those by Spanish designer Manolo Blahnik, whose strappy sandals were so famous that they were stolen from *Sex and the City* protagonist Carrie Bradshaw in an episode where she was mugged at gunpoint. Blahnik was also revered for flirty mules, many of which were historically inspired and incorporated elements of Rococo design.

Transparent loafers, **c. 1955.**
Designed by Beth Levine, American, 1914–2006,
for Herbert Levine Inc., American, founded 1949.
Vinyl upper, leather sole, and acrylic heel.

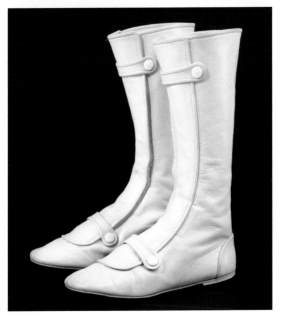

***Boots**, c. 1967.*
Designed by André Courrèges, French, 1923–2016.
Kid-leather.

***Loafer*, Spring 1969.**
Designed by André Courrèges, French, 1923–2016.
Patent leather upper with brass ornament.

***Racecar shoe*, 1965.**
Designed by Katharina Denzinger, German, 1930–2019,
for Herbert Levine Inc., American, founded 1949.
Patent leather, polyvinyl chloride, and polyurethane.

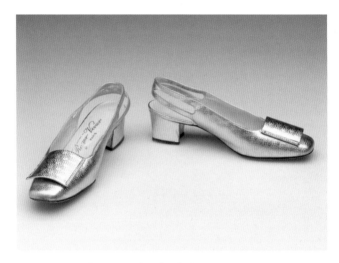

Belle Vivier slingback shoes, **late 1960s.**
Designed by Roger Vivier, French, 1907–1998,
for Saks Fifth Avenue, American, founded 1924.
Gilt-leather embellished with rhinestones.

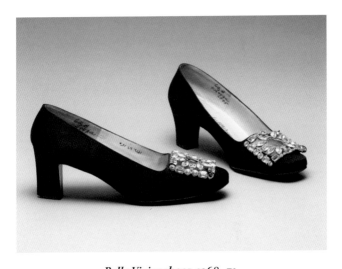

Belle Vivier shoes, 1968–71.
Designed by Roger Vivier, French, 1907–1998.
Silk satin with metal and rhinestone buckle.

Pumps, **c. 1973.**
Designed by Beth Levine, American, 1914–2006,
for Herbert Levine Inc., American, founded 1949.
Patent leather upper with clear Lucite heel.

Platform shoes, **1970–72.**
Greca, American. Multicolored leather;
covered platform and heel.

***Platform sandals**, c. 1972.*
Pelican Footwear NYC, American, 1971–74.
Synthetic-satin upper; polyurethane platform
decorated with vinyl and paint.

Platform shoes, 1972–73.
Raphael, Italian. Metallic-leather upper;
wood platform and heel.

Platform shoes, c. 1975.
Gösta, possibly French. Patent leather upper
and covered platform.

***Platform shoes**, 1970s.*
English. Cotton-velvet upper and covered
heel with silver buckle.

Lace-up boots, c. 1975.
Designed by Jerry Edouard for Kaufmann's, American.
Suede upper with cotton embroidery
and stacked-wood heel.

***Boots,* c. 1968.**
Designed by Beth Levine, American, 1914–2006,
designed for Herbert Levine Inc., American, founded 1949.
Leather upper and shaft.

***Boot tights*, early 1980s.**
Designed by Donna Karan, American, b. 1948, for
Anne Klein and Co., American, founded 1968.
Viscose, nylon, and elastic-velvet upper; leather sole.

***Evening pumps,* c. 1982.**
Susan Bennis/Warren Edwards, American, 1977–1997.
Tie-dyed and splattered patterned silk upper
and leather sole.

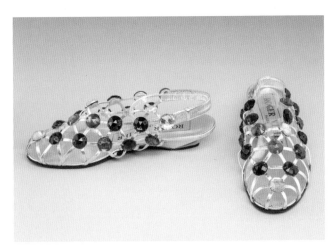

***Sandals**, 1990s.*
Designed by Roger Vivier, French, 1907–1998.
Silver-leather upper decorated with multicolored
foil-backed plastic beads.

Platform evening sandal, 1972.
Biba, British, founded 1963. Satin upper with diamanté
and sequin embellishment on platform and heel.

Pumps, 1991.
Susan Bennis/Warren Edwards, American, 1977–1997.
Silk satin with silk and polyester-chiffon flowers.

***Pumps*, c. 1985.**
Susan Bennis/Warren Edwards, American, 1977–1997.
Painted leather.

***Goya shoes*, Fall/Winter 1986–87.**
Designed by Roger Vivier, French, 1907–1998.
Laser-cut patent leather upper with metal Virgule heel.

***Pump*, Fall/Winter 1988–89.**
Designed by Isabel Canovas, French, b. 1945.
Silk satin embellished with beads and sequins.

Evening mules, 1990–92.
Designed by Manolo Blahnik, Spanish, b. 1942.
Silk satin.

***Evening pumps,* 1990–92.**
Designed by Manolo Blahnik, Spanish, b. 1942.
Silk satin with rhinestone adornment.

***Anglomania platform lace-up shoes*, Fall 1993.**
Designed by Vivienne Westwood, British, b. 1941. Tartan-silk
twill and black patent leather.

Platform pumps, 1990.
Designed by Vivienne Westwood, British, b. 1941.
Embossed leather.

Thorn sandals, **Spring/Summer 1993.**
Designed by Roger Vivier, French, 1907–1998,
for Delman, American, founded 1919. Silk upper
with metal heel and closure.

***Tabi boots,* c. 1990.**
Designed for Maison Margiela, Belgian, founded 1989.
Painted leather with cotton lining; metal
and cord fasteners.

***Stilettos*, Spring 1998.**
Designed by Tom Ford, American, b. 1961, for Gucci,
Italian, founded 1921. Patent leather upper
with metal-spike heel.

***Sandals*, Fall 1991.**
Designed by Yves Saint Laurent, French, 1936–2008.
Satin upper and covered heel with
stacked-rubber platform sole.

***Sandals*, Spring/Summer 1991.**
Designed by Gianni Versace, Italian, 1946–1997.
Printed-silk upper with leather sole.

***Mules*, c. 1996.**
Designed by Manolo Blahnik, Spanish, b. 1942.
Printed synthetic-twill upper with leather sole.

***Lace-up sandal*, Spring 1998.**
Designed by Todd Oldham, American, b. 1961.
Silver metallic leather and clear plastic.

***Circus stiletto boots,* c. 1997.**
Designed by Manolo Blahnik, Spanish, b. 1942. Metallic-lamé
upper with metal-spike heel and velvet laces.

CHAPTER EIGHT
21st Century

The new millennium ushered in an age of technology that revolutionized the design and production of footwear. The internet not only transformed the shopping experience, but encouraged the virtual consumption of shoes—old and new—through social media. With this phenomenon, the enthusiasm for conceptual designs eventually gave way to a new appreciation for shoes as works of art—leading to interdisciplinary design collaborations with visual artists.

The Dutch shoe company United Nude was founded in 2003 by Rem D. Koolhaas and has become known for its unique footwear that exists at the nexus of fashion and architecture. Conceptual designs with an emphasis on structural form have emerged from collaborations with architects such as Zaha Hadid and fashion innovators like Iris van Herpen. Many contemporary shoe designers have gravitated toward the use of metallic elements in their concept designs—which reflects the inherent futurism underlying the integration of new technologies in footwear production. Innovations like 3D printing have played a part in fabricating soles and heels, while digital printing has become central to producing vibrant textiles for fabric uppers. The most forward-thinking designers have challenged traditional notions of form and function in footwear—dispensing with wearability and instead creating shoes more akin to sculptural artworks. Even Manolo Blahnik—the leader of a highly profitable brand—takes delight in creating more experimental works that are "free from commercial restraints."

Shoes in the twenty-first century continue to explore notions of sexuality and power. Styles featuring rock studs, black patent leather, and daggerlike heels simultaneously convey elements of danger and empowerment, while the return of the platform sole elevates the wearer to domineering heights. Notable are the transparent platform Pleaser shoes often worn by sex workers, which recall the chopines worn by Venetian courtesans from the fifteenth to seventeenth centuries. Heeled shoes have generally increased in height, and daringly designed stilettos further accentuate the sensual posture and swinging gait created by an elevated heel. Christian Louboutin pushed this idea to the extreme with his Fetish Ballerine pumps, which create the illusion of a lengthened leg line by forcing the foot into a vertical position.

Louboutin has become the leading name in luxury footwear, and his signature red soles a conspicuous shorthand for affluence. First created in 1993 when the designer painted the bottom of a prototype using red nail polish, the red sole was officially trademarked following multiple legal disputes in several countries. Thus, the Louboutin signature sole continues in the tradition of the talon rouge in the French court—as a prominent marker of status and exclusivity. Well-established footwear brands continue to cash in on their label's prominence by drawing upon design heritage, while simultaneously updating their product for a new generation of customers. For example, reimagined versions of the Ferragamo F-heel continue to walk the brand's runway shows, while the distinctive jeweled ball of Roger Vivier's Boule heel—originally designed in 1953 for actress Marlene Dietrich—remains a consistent element in the brand's recent offerings. Inheriting the apparent legacy of Ferragamo and Vivier are young designers like Nicholas Kirkwood, who launched his first shoe collection in 2005. He quickly emerged at the forefront of the field with his experimental designs and exquisite craftsmanship.

Pleaser platform shoe, 2001.
Pleaser, American, founded 1993. Clear plastic.

***Illusion sandals**, Spring/Summer 2003.*
Designed by Helmut Lang, Austrian, b. 1956. Synthetic upper
with patent leather heel and ankle strap.

Boots, 2005.
Designed by Jimmy Choo, British, born 1948.
Leather upper with stiletto heel and
center-back zipper closure.

Glitter boots, 2005.
Miu Miu, Italian, founded 1993.
Silver-glitter upper with laced front and stiletto heel.

Wedge pumps, 2005.
Prada, Italian, founded 1913.
Metallic leather.

***Open-toe pumps*, Spring 2006.**
Designed by Stefano Pilati, Italian, b. 1965,
for YSL Rive Gauche, French, founded 1966.
Gold-metallic leather.

Dot boots, 2002.
Designed by Damien Hirst, British, b. 1965, manufactured
by Manolo Blahnik, Spanish, born 1942.
Printed-cotton upper with leather sole.

Cantilever pumps, **Spring/Summer 2008.**
Designed by Marc Jacobs, American, b. 1963.
Patent leather.

***Studded sandals*, Spring/Summer 2003.**
Dolce & Gabbana, Italian, founded 1985.
Leather upper with metal studs.

Bhutan no-heel wedge, **Spring/Summer 2006.**
Designed by Manolo Blahnik, Spanish, b. 1942.
Leather upper with metal fastenings.

Pompidou sandals, 2004.
Designed by Beatrix Ong, British, founded 2002.
Silk-covered sole with Swarovski-crystal straps.

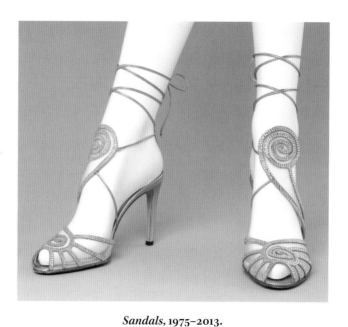

Sandals, 1975–2013.
Valentino S.p.A., Italian, founded 1960. Clear-plastic mesh
embellished with rhinestones; metallic-leather laces.

Stiletto pumps with ankle straps, c. 2008.
Designed by Christian Louboutin, French, b. 1963.
Silk satin upper with suede-covered platform and
patent leather–covered heel.

***Fetish Ballerine pumps*, 2007.**
Designed by Christian Louboutin, French, b. 1963.
Patent leather.

***Armadillo shoe*, Spring/Summer 2010.**
Designed by Alexander McQueen, British, 1969–2010.
Shagreen leather (*Pastinachus sephen*).

Lady Bloom heel-less platform shoes, 2013.
Designed by Noritaka Tatehana, Japanese, b. 1985.
Tooled leather with metallic paint.

Sneaker pumps, 2007.
Designed by Yohji Yamamoto, Japanese, b. 1943, for Adidas,
German, founded 1949. Leather upper with rubber sole.

Platform mules, 2008.
Chanel, French, founded 1910. Clear-vinyl upper decorated
with metal grommets; silver metallic textured patent leather
platform and black patent leather insole.

Mojito shoes, 2015.
Designed by Julian Hakes, British. 3D printed and
injection-molded carbon fiber with leather
lining and rubber sole.

Invisible Naked shoes, 2011.
Designed by Andreia Chaves, Brazilian.
Leather pump with 3D printed exoskeleton.

***Flame mules*, Spring/Summer 2012.**
Prada, Italian, founded 1913.
Patent leather with metal-spike heel.

***Lipstick heel pumps*, Spring 2013.**
Alberto Guardiani, Italian, founded 1947.
Patent leather upper with metal and plastic heel.

***NOVA shoes*, 2013.**
Designed by Zaha Hadid, British-Iraqi, 1950–2016, for United
Nude, Dutch, founded 2013. Chrome-plated vinyl and rubber-
270 blend, injection molded and vacuum cast; fiberglass platform.

Synethesia ankle boots, **Fall/Winter 2010.**
Designed by Iris van Herpen, Dutch, b. 1984,
for United Nude, Dutch, founded 2013.
Kid-leather with metallized strips.

***Ankle boots,* 2011.**
Designed by Alexander McQueen, British, 1969–2010.
Suede upper embellished with gold-crystal studs;
zip fastening with signature skull zipper pull.

***Evening shoes with Boule heel,* Spring 2017.**
Roger Vivier, French, founded 1937. Silk satin upper embellished
with sequins; rhinestone-pavé ball.

Arta sandals, 2015.
Designed by Paul Andrew, English, b. 1979.
Patent leather with decorative multicolored tassels.

***Platform peep-toe stilettos*, 2011.**
Designed by Nicholas Kirkwood, British, b. 1980.
Lace upper with leather-covered platform and heel; suede laces.

***Platform sandal*, Spring 2009.**
Designed by Nicholas Kirkwood, British, b. 1980.
Metallic leather with straps of gold chain and electrical wire.

***Wedge shoes*, Spring 2013.**
Designed by Nicholas Kirkwood, British, b. 1980.
Metallic-leather and suede upper with metal wedge heel.

Riri sandals, 2013.
Designed by Sophia Webster, British, b. 1985.
Multicolored leather and synthetic beads.

Patent Rockstud caged pump, 2020.
Valentino S.p.A., Italian, founded 1960.
Napa-leather upper with platinum-finished studs.

Medusa Aeternitas platform sandals, **Spring 2021.**
Versace, Italian, founded 1978.
Calf leather with golden-bangle ankle strap.

Platform croc, **Spring/Summer 2018.**
Balenciaga, Spanish, founded 1919. Molded resin.

Index of Names

Photo Credits

Project Editors: Lauren Bucca and Colette Laroya
Proofreader: Ashley Benning
Cover Design: Misha Beletsky
Design: Ada Rodriguez
Production Manager: Louise Kurtz

First edition
10 9 8 7 6 5 4 3 2 1

ISBN 978-0-7892-1414-0

Library of Congress Cataloging-in-Publication Data available upon request

For bulk and premium sales and for text adoption procedures, write to
Customer Service Manager, Abbeville Press, Inc., 655 Third Avenue, New York,
NY 10017, or call 1-800-Artbook.

Visit Abbeville Press online at www.abbeville.com.

SELECTED TINY FOLIOS™ FROM ABBEVILLE PRESS